A Snake
in the
Bathtub

A Snake
in the
Bathtub

by Curt Brummett

illustrations by Wendell E. Hall

August House Publishers, Inc.

LITTLE ROCK

Printed in the United States of America
10 9 8 7 6 5 4 3 2 1

LIBRARY OF CONGRESS CATALOGING-IN-PUBLICATION
DATA

Brummett, Curt
A snake in the bathtub / by Curt Brummett : illustrations by Wendell E.
Hall. — 1st August House ed.
p.   cm.
"First published by Maverick Books, Inc., 1990"—T.P. verso.
ISBN 0-87483-169-5 (acid-free) : $6.95
1. Southwest, New—Social life and customs—Humor. 2. Brummett,
Curt—Childhood and youth—Humor.
I. Hall, Wendell E. II. Title.
F787.B78   1991
979—dc20   91-6572

First published by Maverick Books, Inc., 1990
First August House edition, 1991

All these stories appeared first and in different form in *Livestock Weekly*
between January and November of 1985. Several of them also appeared in
Horse and Rider.

Executive: Liz Parkhurst
Project editor: Judith Faust
Cover design and illustrations: Wendell E. Hall
Typography: Lettergraphics, Little Rock

This book is printed on archival-quality paper which meets the
guidelines for performance and durability of the Committee on
Production Guidelines for Book Longevity of the
Council on Library Resources.

AUGUST HOUSE, INC.   PUBLISHERS   LITTLE ROCK

For Sheila Madge—Maw—
the Little Woman—Mammy.
(There are four names here, but they all apply
to the same woman: my wife!)

Introduction

Several years ago I was asked to speak at a writers' workshop in the Dallas area. The writers who attended were all children, from first grade on through high school. Many of them had already written stories and were seeking information about how to get them published.

On the surface, this seemed a splendid idea: encouraging kids to write at an early age and teaching them that they could be writers even though they were from Texas instead of New York.

But there was something about it that bothered me. What I wanted most to say to these kids—and to their mothers—was that there is more to writing than putting words down on a piece of paper. Good writers don't write words; they write stories.

I wanted to tell them, "I'm glad you're writing a novel in the third grade, and I hope you're having fun, but don't worry about getting published until you have something to say. Mozart had something to say in the third grade, but most of us don't. We need to do a lot more living. We need to acquire wisdom, humility, and a sense of humor. A good story contains those qualities."

That's not the kind of advice most young writers, or even older writers, want to hear. We live in the land of instant hamburgers and instant pizza, and it's only natural that we would think of writing in the same terms: "Gimme a three-hundred-page novel with a strong female lead and television tie-in, and hold the onions!"

But the most serious challenge that faces the beginning writer is not getting his work published, although that is the one we hear most about. The toughest part of being a writer is acquiring the kind of stories that provide nourishment for the human spirit.

People need good stories just as they need wholesome food and clean water. They need stories that bring form and order to everyday experience. They need stories that affirm fundamental human values, stories that allow the reader to laugh out loud and perhaps even to shed a few tears.

Finding that kind of story is not an easy task. It takes a lot of living, and the writer shouldn't expect to get it without paying a price. People often ask me how long it took me to write my first *Hank the Cowdog* book. Well, I had observed dogs for some thirty years, had been writing for fifteen, and had worked as ranch cowboy for eight before I ever wrote the first word.

With that behind me, I wrote the story in four weeks. Writing the words was the easy part. Finding the words that told a good story was the hard part.

This brings us to the present volume of stories by Curt Brummett. It must have been sometime in 1987 that I first read one of his stories. When I finished, I said to myself, "If this fellow lives long enough, he's going to become a very important writer."

I figured he must be at least seventy-five years old, dried up, crippled, toothless, hawk-eyed, and leather-faced. Anybody with the kind of experience Brummett was packing into those yarns had to be at least seventy-five.

I met the old geezer for the first time in June of 1989 at the Texas Tech National Symposium on the Cowboy, and I was shocked to find that he was only forty years old. I couldn't believe it. How could anyone his age have so many extraordinary stories to tell?

By design or by accident, Brummett lived a story-creating kind of existence long before he decided to write about it. Stories first, writing second. He had a lot to say because he had done so many interesting things.

As you will see in the stories, he started out as an ornery little snot of a kid who should have been drowned at an early age. Having survived that, he became a ranch cowboy, a feedlot cowboy, a semiprofessional roper, a roughneck, a tool pusher, and a firefighter. He has also worked a shift as Sheila's husband, as the father of three girls, and now as a grandfather.

Brummett doesn't write the kind of gloomy tale that announces the death of the American West, including the cowboy and all his values. His stories announce that the West is bursting with life and laughter, and one reason it lives is that we have people like Brummett around who keep renewing it with their sweat and blood.

The West is ultimately a state of mind. We keep it alive by living it. We renew it each day with love and sacrifice, and the best of our writing about it is fueled by the integrity of that experience.

You'll find that in the work of Elmer Kelton, J. Evetts Haley, Spike Van Cleve, Fay Ward, Ben Green, Ace Reid, Charlie Russell, Baxter Black, and a few others. And you'll find it here in Curt's book. Every time Brummett writes a sentence, he makes the West a stronger, better, and more enjoyable place.

Several years ago I had lunch with an old rancher, and he was telling me about a man he admired. I'll never forget the way he put it: "He still has the smell of the fire on him."

I will borrow that high compliment and use it to describe Curt Brummett's stories: They still have the smell of the fire on them.

This is Curt's first book, but it certainly won't be his last. Remember his name, because we'll be seeing a lot of it in years to come.

John R. Erickson

Contents

Chapter One

The Suicidal Heifer

Many times I have asked myself why it is always the youngest of the crew, the newest member of the team, or the most gullible guy that gets the nasty, dirty, or even dangerous jobs that nobody else wants.

I'm speaking from experience, because when I was a kid, I was instructed to do things that even a seasoned Green Beret would have backed off from.

Kind of like the time Dear Old Dad's favorite yearling heifer got into the steer pasture.

As far as the Old Man was concerned, this Brahman-cross heifer was the solution to the making of a perfect breed. He commented once that if he had to, he would pawn Ma and me off on the neighbors and sell his favorite cutting horse just to feed her.

Me and a buddy of mine had been checking some water gaps on the northwest side of the steer pasture and was on our way back to the house when we spotted this heifer about two hundred yards from the gate. The only problem was, she was two hundred into the wrong pasture. The gate was closed so we figured she crawled through somewhere and we just needed to put her back where she belonged.

Well, the first thing we thought of was to rope and stretch her out a time or two and then show her the home pasture. But us being the sensible type ranch kids we were, we decided to drive her to the gate and put her back in the gentle way. Boy, Dad would sure be proud of us.

In the country where I was raised, there are certain things you learn at a very early age. One is that the only thing dumber than a cow is a black cow, whether it's crossed with any other color or not. And the only thing dumber than a black cow is somebody (anybody) who tries to work just one. That's one rule that's held true all my life.

We knew where we wanted her to go. She knew where we wanted her to go. The problem was, she didn't care nothing about going, least not where we wanted her. She left out with one thing in mind, and that was to go anywhere but there.

Now, my little horse was pretty fast and he could cow better than most. Terry's horse was some better than mine in the cow department but not quite as fast. Even with the combination of us and our horses, we couldn't get her to drive.

After about five minutes, we had succeeded in several things: we had lost a half a mile of country, we had made ourselves and our horses mad, and we had considerably aggravated a black crossbreed heifer.

I remembered another rule. "If it don't drive, pen, or pay attention, rope it, choke it, and show it home is a nice place to be."

Terry and me had our ropes down and was fixing to attack when three of the cowboys working for my dad

came over the hill and seen us. It was a couple of minutes later that I figured out that being a kid had its drawbacks.

Well, Bob seen what was going on and figured out right quick what the trouble was. He explained in pretty harsh terms that a couple of dumb kids shouldn't be messing with something they didn't know anything about.

Me being the quiet type, then as I am now, I took my chewing out, and then I told him since he knew so much about it, he could put her back in the heifer pasture and me and Terry would just sit back and learn.

The only thing them boys got done that we didn't was to get her mad enough to fight everybody. Course, we got the blame for this, too.

They finally decided to rope her and lead her home.

Terry and me was told to stay out of the way, and Bob and Andy roped her and headed for the gate.

After the setting straight I got, the only thing I could hope for was the old man to show up and catch Bob with his rope on that special heifer.

I could just picture Bob agreeing with Dad about how sorry cowboys really are. All they want to do is rope a man's cattle instead of working. And how they would rather run the fat off a good cow instead of working her the gentle way. And all this time I would just set back and agree and grin. Yep, I sure would have liked to see someone else get their pedigree read besides me.

We got her through the gate, got the gate closed, and turned her loose. That mutton-headed idiot went plumb crazy. She jumped up, ran under one horse, and headed for the gate.

Seems she had it in mind to jump it instead of run through it. That was the only sensible thing she had done all afternoon.

It was kinda pretty, for a minute anyway. It was just that she left the ground about five feet too soon. When she hit the gate, she looked like a wet towsack that had been thrown against a wall.

I guess all the excitement messed up her ability to judge distance.

When I realized she had broke her neck and was permanently dead, I got a very clear picture of my future.

I would be locked in the cellar, fed bread and water, and left to sleep on the hide of the finest cow critter that ever lived. I'd have to sleep on that hide so's I would be reminded that I caused the prevention of the advancement of the entire cattle industry.

Bob cut her throat, and as he started dressing her out, he told Terry and me to go get the pickup and explain to my dad how we caused her to get excited and commit suicide. And since she was so excited and hot, the meat probably wouldn't be any good.

Now if you want to talk suicide, just walk up and break some bad news to my old man. I figured my life expectancy was about two minutes longer than it would take to ride to the house and tell my dad the story of the suicidal heifer.

I would sooner pregnancy test a mountain lion than to get him mad at me.

Dad saw us riding in and met us at the barn. He greeted us cheerful enough and asked how our day went. When I tried to tell him, he cut in.

"You know that heifer I was so high on? Well, I rode out this morning and looked at her real close, and you know what I decided to do? She's too goofy to make a momma out of, so I just put her in the steer pasture. The next time we're out there and she's handy, we can bring her in to the pens and fatten her up for a beef. I had to rope her and drag her through the gate. Then I had to jerk her down three or four times just so's I could get my rope off. She was plenty mad, so I just left her in the steer pasture 'til she calmed down. Yup, she's a little dingy."

Hearing how he had changed his mind about her was a little bit of relief on our nerves, and we did get come confidence back.

So we told our story.

The chewing out wasn't near as bad as we thought it would be, but it still hit about four of the Richter scale. I guess it was sort of like stepping out of the fire back into the frying pan.

We butchered her out and she made pretty good beef, but every time I took a bite of the old silly thing, I swore that if I ever got old enough and anything went wrong, I was going to see to it the nearest kid got the blame for it.

Chapter Two

It Don't Take Much Dynamite to Blow Up an Outhouse

One day in 1959 while me and Terry were exploring the canyons to the northeast of the Canadian River, we found a gold mine. Well, we figured it would be if we could just get the hole started.

But after we spent three weeks working with pick, shovel, tamping bar, and tin cup, we figured a little dynamite would help. So on Sunday we rode over to the local well driller's house. Since he wasn't there to ask, we helped ourselves to the dynamite and put two sticks apiece inside our shirts.

After we were about halfway home, we kinda got worried about where we was gonna keep this stuff. Since we had gotten in trouble for stealing our dads' home brew and hiding it here and there, we didn't have any decent hiding places left. Besides that, if we was gone for more than two hours, our dads started checking on us.

We were trying like crazy to figure out where a couple of fifth-grade boys should store their dynamite when we both came up with the same idea. It was such a simple

solution, we were surprised we hadn't been using it before.

We stored our supplies in the outhouse behind the community clubhouse. We knew it would be safe there.

On Sunday afternoon, the only activity in that little New Mexico town was at the preacher's house, and that was only if they had someone over to dinner. Anyway, we slipped into town, stashed the loot, and made good our escape. Not even the town mutt knew we had been there.

Since neither of us knew anything about dynamite, we decided to bring in a professional. Course, that meant we would have to cut him in on the gold mine. There was only one person that was smart enough to help us and at the same time could still be trusted.

We decided we would talk to him at school the next day.

Yup, Larry was pretty smart, but he had one big downfall. Two, actually. He was semi-greedy, and he could be talked into anything.

The next day on our lunch hour, we conned Larry into going over to the poolhall for a soda pop. After we casually mentioned our gold mine and the fact that we might take in a pardner, things picked up considerable.

It wasn't but a matter of seconds before Larry had pledged total secrecy and even offered to supply soda pop and such if we would just take him in as a pardner.

We studied his proposal for a couple of minutes and then told him we would let him in, but everything had to be kept a secret. And since he was a pardner now, we figured we could show him our storehouse and maybe get his views on what else we might need.

He liked to have had a smothering spell when he saw the dynamite, and he came pretty near to backing out. Some smooth and fast talking changed his mind. Actually, it was simple logic. We just explained to him that if he quit, we would mention to the principal that we just might know who smeared the white Karo syrup on the toilet seats in the girls' restroom.

He did throw a fit at that statement. He screamed that he was innocent and we knew it. All he had done was watch the hall while we did the smearing.

We had to agree with him, but he had to admit that it was our word against his. After all, it would be two against one.

What he failed to realize was that the principal wouldn't have believed Terry and me if we'd told him that bears had hair.

After Larry finally calmed down, we headed back to school. He told us we would need some blasting caps to go with the dynamite and he thought he could get some.

He outdid hisself that evening. His mother had to come in for a meeting at the clubhouse to help plan for the spring carnival. He begged her to let him go with her and she did. After supper, he slipped out to his dad's tool shed and got some blasting caps and a small keg of black powder.

He figured since his dad was finished enlarging some of their stock watering holes, he wouldn't miss them.

Larry put the caps and powder in the back seat of the car and covered them with a blanket. After he and his mother got to the clubhouse, he waited for the right time and then sneaked them out to the storehouse.

Boy, was we surprised when he showed us the extra supplies! Yup, we decided to make him a full pardner.

Everything was set. The coming weekend we would all meet a-horseback, go to the canyons, and blow ourselves to riches. We would be the only three kids in the country with new saddles and silver-mounted bits—not to mention an unlimited supply of soda pop.

But before that could come to pass, we had to attend the spring carnival. Everyone in the community had been planning on that carnival for quite some time. There was only four things in our part of the world that could get everyone together at one time: a wedding, a funeral, the Thanksgiving-Christmas festival, and spring carnival.

The spring carnival required total involvement from everyone—making the decorations, baking pies and cakes, fixing salads, and barbecuing a beef and several goats. There'd be free soda pop, punch, coffee, and tea, and of course the men'd generally have a jug or two outside. There'd be games for kids and adults and everyone always had a good time. We were all ready for the carnival this year.

Friday night came on time, and everyone headed for the clubhouse. It was raining when we got there, and there was some pretty bad lightning back off in the west, but it looked like it would probably blow over.

Terry and me located each other right off and started planning our next two days. Larry and his family got there about thirty minutes later, and he was sure excited.

"Come on! Boy, have I got something to show y'all."

We followed him outside. There, bundled up nice and neat in the trunk of the car, was a Coleman lantern and five gallons of white gas. He figured we could use the light after we had blasted our way into the gold mine.

We wasted no time putting that stuff with the rest of our supplies, and then we headed back to the party.

It was about nine o'clock when the wind really got to blowing and the lightning started getting wilder and wilder. There was no one particularly worried about it, because the party would probably outlast the storm.

Terry and me was getting worried, though, mainly because if the rain kept up, we would have to fix water gaps the next day instead of going to our gold mine.

It was along about then that our mining empire got blown plumb out of proportion. It seems lightning hit our warehouse.

K A—*B O O M ! !*

It was a terrifying thing. There was babies crying, women screaming, and dogs barking in the street. There was also a bunch of men that had never sobered up so quick in their lives.

Someone finally got enough nerve to look out what was left of the back door and see what had really happened. Actually, there wasn't all that much to see except a little fire and a hole in the ground you could have parked a B-52 in.

Half of the old maple tree was gone, and the outhouse had just disappeared. I mean, there wasn't no kindling, no *nothing* left.

One old man said, "That must have been one heck of a bolt of lightning."

Another said, "One! That must have been four or five bolts of lightning, all at the same time."

Of course, my Dear Old Dad had to help by saying the only thing *he* had ever seen make something just plain disappear like that was either dynamite or blasting powder.

That's when Larry got caught crawling out the front door, and Terry and me noticed that we had about half of the multitude staring at us. Things was looking dim.

The old well driller got our dads off to one side, and after a short discussion, they called us over.

There was one rule we boys never broke: we never lied to our dads, because if we did and got caught, we were likely to get beat near to death, not to mention getting our horses taken away.

So when they asked us about the driller's dynamite and where we had put it, we admitted to everything.

I had never heard talk of kids being lynched until that night. I even heard a few comments about how all three of us might be mentally unbalanced.

After a short discussion, we decided to disband the mining company and concentrate all our energies on a new challenge. It seems public opinion had sort of decreed we should replace that outhouse with our own money.

Chapter Three

Revenge at the Girls' Latrine

The summer of 1959 was a trying period of time in my life. It all started when Terry's folks got with my folks and discussed our religious upbringing.

They decided that a two-week stretch in church camp would do us some good. We would be away from all those foul-mouth cowboys who seemed to be giving us silly ideas, and we would be associated with Normal Children. Surely in two weeks we could pick up some kind of decent thinking.

Well, they broke the news to us, and in spite of our begging and pleading, it was set. D-Day came, and we were a little confused. Couldn't figure whether we were being sent away because we were unwanted and unloved, or whether they were trying one last shot at getting us started on the right path. We decided it was a little of both.

After a long and dull trip, we arrived at camp. It was up in the high country, as pretty a place as you would ever want to see. All the cabins and the girls' dorm were built out of logs, and they all had fireplaces.

Terry and me stayed in a cabin with three other kids. When Terry unrolled his bedroll, he exposed a big sack of homemade peanut brittle. At this time, he let me pass out a very small chunk to each of the three boys.

When they asked for more, we mentioned that for a nickel a piece, they could have all they wanted. We thought that was a good business idea, but one of them kids went and told that we was selling candy.

We not only lost our candy, we got a twenty-minute talk about how it was better to give than to receive. And at the end of the discussion, we were sent to gather firewood for our cabin.

Gathering firewood up there was like a paid vacation. There was a man hired to cut and haul all the wood, and he dumped it about fifty yards behind the cabin, which made it pretty nice.

After our first trip to the woodpile, it started a slow rain, and us being ranch kids, we figured we'd better haul some more firewood. We knew wet wood don't burn too good, and we wanted plenty to keep warm by.

By suppertime, it had rained almost four inches and showed no sign of letting up. As we ate in the big dining room, we heard a couple of the adults griping about not having any dry wood, and how cold it would be if they couldn't get that wet wood to burn.

Terry and I had the same thought at the same time.

After supper, we made it back to the cabin ahead of the others and started plotting our next business venture.

We figured we would charge a dollar a cabin to get a fire going and show 'em how to keep it going and dry out more wood at the same time.

We asked permission to go to the latrine, and when we left our cabin, we went to the cabin next to ours. They had made several attempts to start a fire, with no results.

The adult for that cabin had gone to get some more paper and advice.

We made our proposition and they accepted. I slipped a piece of dry wood out from under my jacket and Terry brought out the old T-shirt he had gotten from his suitcase. Those town kids were amazed that a few shavings of dry wood and a piece of old T-shirt and one match could get a fire going.

We left them with a few instructions on fire-tending and also on how it wasn't necessary for the adults in camp to know that we were charging for our services. In fact, we pointed out helpfully, anybody who squealed on us might regret it.

So we collected our dollar and went to the next cabin. Out of twelve cabins, we made four dollars and a full two-weeks' supply of dessert. Most of those kids sure was glad we'd showed up. Most, but not all.

Some of the girls tattled on us. The next morning at breakfast, Terry and I noticed we were being surrounded by adults, and I mean a bunch of adults, about fifteen or twenty of them. And behind them stood several righteous-looking, smart-faced girls.

After a lengthy discussion and chewing, they sentenced us to be confined in the wood-hauler's cabin. We would be escorted to and from classes by an adult, and when everyone else was enjoying plenty of recreation, we would be working in the kitchen.

We would be escorted to and from the latrine, to and from the showers, to and from the woodpile, and we would lose our rights to go to the concession stand.

We did like our dads had told us, and just as we had done a million times before. When we got caught messing up, we took our punishment like men, and there was no begging for mercy.

But the thought did come to mind that we might want to get some revenge on those tattletale girls.

We got our bedrolls and clothes and were escorted to the wood-hauler's cabin. His name was Zeke and he seemed pretty old. He explained the situation to us, short and sweet:

"As long as you little troublemakers stay in line, we'll get along fine, but the first time either of you messes up, I'll wear my belt out on your narrow little butts. Now, if there's any questions, ask 'em. If there's not, say your prayers and get to bed."

We assured him there were no questions. We went to bed.

The next morning Zeke went off early and left us alone waiting for our adult escort. It was in this short unsupervised span that I explained my plan for revenge. Terry loved it and said he had a plan of his own. We compared and decided to use both.

When we were escorted to the kitchen to help get ready for supper, I slipped a quart jar of mineral oil under my jacket. I had no idea why Zeke kept it around, but I was sure that I needed it more than he did.

Just before supper was ready, I glanced over at Terry and saw him put a whole roll of that clear plastic you cover dishes with under his shirt. Just then the cooks rang the dinner bell.

About halfway through supper, Terry asked for permission to go to the latrine. Since he was going by himself, and most of the adults were busy, the cook told him to go ahead.

He was gone about thirty minutes, and I was starting to get worried when he finally came back in. He just grinned and nodded.

That's when I started my plan.

I grabbed a big pitcher of chocolate milk and poured about half of it into the sink. Then I poured the mineral oil into the pitcher and stirred it up. Then I went straight to the table where the blabbermouth girls were sitting.

They snickered at me and made faces. I set the full pitcher down and picked up the empty one and went back to the kitchen.

After supper, me and Terry were replaced by a couple of other convict-boys who had been caught messing up. We were escorted back to Zeke's cabin and told to write letters to our parents. And since we were still grounded, we couldn't go to the campfire and sing with the others. Big deal.

After half an hour or so, Zeke said he had to go the office and that he would be back in about fifteen minutes. He asked if we knew what he would do to us if we so much as sneezed before he got back. We said, "Yes, sir," and he went out the door.

That's when we heard two or three muffled screams, and the sound of people running.

Zeke told us not to move and left out in the direction of the screams, which seemed to be coming from the girls' latrine.

In a little while, Zeke came back, chuckling to himself. We asked what all the screams were about. He said the meatloaf that we'd had for supper had disagreed with five or six of the girls, and they'd all headed for the latrine at the same time.

There they discovered that somebody had slipped in and covered the toilet seats with clear plastic. All six toilets. And, to add insult to injury, somebody had drained the hot water tanks in both the boys' and girls' showers.

"Yep," Zeke chuckled, "whoever did that, if they get caught, is sure gonna see a dark day in Hard Rock."

We wasn't too worried about Hard Rock, wherever that was, because we had just pulled off the perfect payback.

About 11:30 there was a loud banging on the door. Zeke jumped out of bed and went to the door, hollering for whoever it was to calm down and just tell him what they wanted.

Now, Terry and me was used to unexpected failure, and we had an idea of what they might want. By three seconds after that door was opened, we knew for sure.

Our hides.

After about two hours of screaming and hollering, they decided they would ship us home. The main adult leader asked Zeke if he would take us. He said he would if our parents'd met him halfway.

We didn't know which would be worse, riding the first half with a self-confessed child-beater or riding the second half with our dads, who had reputations of their own and plenty of time to work up a good mad.

Before we left the next morning, the camp leaders made us apologize to the girls we had poisoned and offended. We didn't want to, but we did.

We told 'em how sorry we were and not to forget what happened to snotty little girls who tattled on Terry and Curt.

Chapter Four

Gastronomical Endeavors
Won and Lost

The main topic of this little story is gas. Not unleaded or ethanol or even regular—just plain gas.

Where I was raised, you didn't mention anything about gas. And if the occasions should come to be noticed, you excused the problem and then slid out of the room with a red face.

When it comes to gas, there seems to be a double standard. When you're with the boys, gas can create some highly competitive times. When you happen to be around a bunch of girls or some of them really radical church women, you have to be fully awake and on your toes.

One time Terry and I spent the night over at Larry's. It was a Saturday in the summer, the first day in quite a while that our folks had let us get together for more than two or three minutes at a time.

We ran and ripped all day, played world champion ropers on the milk pen calves, and managed not to get into any trouble. That evening, as we were helping Larry with his chores, the subject of gas came up. Bragging began and was followed by a series of challenges. It appeared we had just talked ourselves into a friendly gas war.

In our little area of the world, the main diet consisted of beef, beans, and vegetables. The beans, of course, had a little to do with our kind of competition. As we were finishing with the chores, we made up the rules for the contest. We could eat as much as we wanted of anything but the beans. We each had to eat three helpings of beans. That way each of us would have an equal shot at the title. So to speak.

Well, supper was great, plenty of everything, and the deviled eggs that Larry's mom fixed was probably the best I had ever eaten. Little did I know that after eating eight or nine along with three helpings of beans, I was fixing to acquire a championship title I would never lose.

When we finished eating, we went out to play some basketball, and after a while, Larry's dad hollered for us to come on in and get our baths and get to bed. He didn't want a bunch of dirty kids oversleeping and making everyone late for church.

Did he say church?

Good gravy…we had forgotten all about having to go to church, and here we were, fully loaded for the gas war to end all gas wars.

It was a terrible event. There we were, all three of us, in the same bed and with several dense clouds floating around the room. For some reason, I didn't get into the competition until daylight. It seems as though the beans and the eggs worked against each other until about breakfast time.

I excused myself from the table and slipped out the door. I could hear Larry and Terry laughing while Larry's mom chewed them out and explained that at least Curt had the manners to leave the room, and they shouldn't be laughing at someone's embarrassment.

As we pulled up to the church, we could see that just about everyone in the country was there, all the kids we went to school with and most of their parents. There was even that goofy red-headed little girl who had a crush on me.

I don't know what made her like me, but I was stuck with her. She came over to us and said it was gonna be okay if all the kids in the fifth grade sat together because she had already asked her daddy, and he said so. Her daddy was the preacher.

She tried to grab my hand and I just snarled at her. Then she tried to step closer and I did it. I got back in the competition. Lucky for me it got laid off on Terry. I guess it was the way the wind was blowing.

She turned red, he turned red, and I headed for the church house. Larry was almost down on the ground laughing, and I was building pressure.

I began to wonder if I had made a mistake, entering the sweepstakes the night before church. I was trying to avoid any contact with other people, simply because I couldn't tell when the next round was going to start.

My mother called me over and said it was all right if I sat with the little red-headed girl, but there had better not be any talking or laughing. I assured her there would be no talking, but I thought to myself there was a very good possibility of some snickering.

The preacher got up and went to doing his thing. Larry and Terry was sitting behind me and that red-headed girl, and I was starting to suffer. That girl had crowded me 'til I was up against the end of the pew, and Larry and Terry was giggling about it.

I had crossed my legs and started to sweat. Somewhere between the third and fourth hymn, I started getting weak, and that little girl started getting closer. I had all I could do just to stay hooked, when the preacher said, "Let us pray."

Boy, if he only knew.

It was about the time everyone had gotten down to some serious prayer that it happened. That little redheaded female poked me in the ribs. When I jumped from the poke, there was a slippage of gas. Sounded kind of like a two-by-twelve being ripped in half. The silent prayer came to a halt.

I jumped up, looked the little girl square in the eye, and hissed just loud enough for everyone to hear, "*Sherry, couldn't you at least have excused yourself?!*"

With that, I walked around and sat down next to Larry and Terry.

Them two traitors was laughing so hard, they were having minor gas problems theirselves, and I noticed from the corner of my eye some other problems on the way. Our Dear Old Moms were on their feet.

The little red-headed girl stampeded out of the church house, and we boys was sentenced to be separated for life—again. But there was a bright spot. As we waited in the car for church to be over, Larry mentioned that I was now the World Champeen Gas Passer.

Old Tom Was A Good Old Cat

Me and old Tom had a lifestyle similar to that of the Hindenburg. It seemed that every time something went wrong, it was either blamed on me or old Tom, or both. And after being unjustly accused, we would crash and burn.

Like the time the Old Man was shoeing Spooks. As he was working, old Tom and me was doing our part to rid the world of disease-carrying rodents. We was killing mice.

Dear Old Dad had Spooks crosstied in the hallway of the barn and just about had him calmed down. I guess when Tom and me came tearing into the hallway from the feedroom hot on the trail of a marauding mouse, we kind of startled Dad. When we spooked Dad, Dad spooked Spooks, and Spooks came unglued.

I caught a glancing blow from something that knocked me plumb out the barn door. By the time I quit rolling, got up, and looked inside, all I could see was cat hair, horse hair, and dust. After the hair and dust started to settle, I could see Dad and old Tom holed up in the back of a stall. Each one was trying to get behind the other in order to avoid the feet of old Spooks. I had never heard a cat growl like that and I didn't recognize too many of the things Dad was calling old Tom.

I made myself scarce.

That night at supper, as Dad was explaining the black eye and the cat tracks on his neck, he casually mentioned, "If that cat hadn't made good his escape and hid in the post pile, I'd have clubbed him to death with the hoof nippers." Then he said, "Due to that cat, old Spooks will probably never go near the barn again, and he's *shore* gonna be tough to put shoes on from now on."

I was proud that the Old Man didn't see me get knocked out of the barn. With no more than a doubtful look, he accepted my story about tripping and hitting my head on the barn door. And he gave me a dirty look when I asked him why he called old Spooks old Spooks.

Since he didn't know I was with old Tom, I wasn't about to tell him. After all, what he didn't know wouldn't hurt me.

A couple of weeks later, I was doing chores before breakfast when Dad called me back to the house.

It seemed as though there was going to be a discussion on why I had left a tray full of cactus plants on the toilet seat. I don't think he minded me moving my plants, but he sure was upset about where I had left them.

The light bulb was burned out in the bathroom, and it was pretty dark. Since he knew where the toilet was, he started to tend to business anyway. I guess the tray of cactus kind of changed his mind.

He certainly appeared upset. He informed me that since his rear was going to be sore for a while, so was mine. He did not tell an untruth.

When he got through with me, I had lost all interest in breakfast, and limped out to the barn to finish my chores. When I finished, I caught old Tom and we went to the barn loft. Yep, me and old Tom understood each other.

I was standing there holding Tom, thinking how I got the worst end of the discussion, because there wasn't any way that cactus could have raised welts on Dad like he raised on me. It was right then, standing in the hayloft door, that I saw my chance to even up the score.

Now, I was not a violent person, and I never had the nerve to even talk back to my Dear Old Dad. Though I didn't always want to, I always showed respect for the old cuddly thing. So I have no *idea* as to why I did what I did.

Dad and a couple of cowboys came riding around the corner of the barn, heading out to the bull pasture. One was riding a greenbroke colt, the other was riding a goof-proof old ranch horse named Puddin', and Dad was riding Spooks.

I gave old Tom to Dad.

Old Spooks lived up to his name. He jumped sideways so hard and fast the Old Man lost his hat and his cigarettes. This in turn caused a major disturbance with the colt. He jumped to get clear of the horse with the screaming critter on his back, and proceeded to start bucking.

Puddin' stopped to see what all the commotion was about just in time to get run smooth over by a horse and cowboy. The cowboy seemed to be wearing a strange sort of hat.

Old Tom had decided there was entirely too much action on the ground, and he would just stay up with the

Old Man. Dad had a different idea. I guess it's pretty tough to ride a bucking horse and get a scared cat off your head at the same time.

By now the other two cowboys were afoot, and old Spooks was a basket case. The last I saw of them as they went out of sight around the corner of the barn, Spooks was gaining speed, old Tom was losing ground, and the Old Man was still trying to lose old Tom.

The other two cowboys couldn't figure out what got into that goofy cat and was discussing it as they started to catch their horses.

I eased back to the house, content with the score.

About an hour later when Dad came in, he herded Spooks back towards the barn. They made it to within about forty yards and that was as close as that horse was going. Yep, old Spooks was getting paranoid about the barn.

Dad came storming into the house and headed straight for the gun cabinet. His face and shirt looked like he had been drug through a very large pile of barbed wire.

I was starting to get a little worried.

As he was telling Maw about it, he would stop every few words and put in another shell.

"That goofy cat has attacked me for the last time. For no reason at all, he jumped out of the barn loft right on top of me and my horse. He not only clawed the fire out of me, he caused Pete and Howard to get bucked off. And Howard was riding *Puddin'*."

I started to tell him that Howard had got off by hisself when Spooks run over them, but again I figured what he didn't know wouldn't hurt me.

He finished up by saying, "Pete and Howard are OK, but what little brain that horse ever had is so scrambled he won't come in for water for a month. Now that cat is gonna go. Between that cat and that cactus, I am a little upset.

He stormed out the door with the shotgun, blood in his eye.

After I had studied the situation for a minute, I considered telling him what really happened. Then I considered the state of mind of the man with the gun. Then I thought, "Old Tom, better you than me."

Chapter Six

Thing That Go Bump and Hiss in the Night

One time, my folks and I got in late from town, and my dad told me to get the chores done and then check out the old toolshed to see if any of the chickens had been laying eggs in it. I finished up the chores by lantern light and headed to the toolshed.

Now, we hadn't used this old building in several years, and the door wouldn't quite shut because it was blocked with blow sand. There was just enough room for me to squeeze through and not tear my shirt on the splinters in the door.

Most people know how much light an old lantern gives, but for those that don't, I'll tell you. It won't light up a whole toolshed. I had found a few eggs when I heard this very loud, very long *hisssss.* My hair stood straight up. And I was wearing a hat.

I held the lantern a little higher and looked around, but I couldn't see anything. I considered forgetting the eggs and heading for the house, but this wasn't too good an idea because the Old Man had told me to gather the eggs, and unless I had two broke legs and an arm to match, I had better gather them.

I turned to see if I could find any more eggs, and I heard it again. Yep, it was definitely a hiss. My hair nearly pushed my hat off, and I could just about imagine something really big wanting to try it on.

I raised the light as high as I could and started to turn very slowly towards the door. I figured I could just leave out of there as calmly as possible and explain to Dear Old Dad that I just didn't find all that many eggs. As I made my turn to the door, I seen it.

There it was, the single biggest, possibly the longest in the world, and I know for a *fact* the largest-around bullsnake ever seen by a human. He was hanging from a beam and kinda crooked up so he could look me straight in the eye. It shouldn't make any difference that the beam was only six feet off the floor and I was well over four feet tall, but he was still looking me in the eye.

I gave him the eggs and the lantern.

While all of this was going on, Dad got to wondering what was taking me so long, so he came down to the toolshed to find out. It wasn't *my* fault he got to the door at the same time I did. And it wasn't *my* fault he didn't have enough sense to get out of the way when I screamed and ran smooth over that old rotten door and him, too. It might have been my fault that the lantern caught the shed on fire.

After I got calmed down a little, I explained the situation, and he also calmed down. At least this way, all we had to do to haul off that old tool shed was to load up some ashes and scatter them to the wind. And I figured with any luck at all, there would be a barbecued bullsnake somewhere in the mess.

Right after we finally got electric lines run to the homeplace, we had lights in the house, the barn, and even in the bunkhouse. Me being the quiet type, it only took me about two weeks to figure out a new and unique way to drive my Old Man flat up the wall.

All that electric stuff not only brightened up our lives, it helped me stay entertained.

You see, the switch they had put in the barn was some kind of high-tension-type thing. After a couple of weeks, I discovered that if you only pulled it halfway off, the light would go out and in a little while the spring would flip the switch back on.

Of an evening, when I finished the chores, I would just flip the light switch half off and wait for old Dad to jump up and head to the barn, thinking someone was messing around where he shouldn't be.

One night as we were eating supper, the barn light came on. Dad just stayed calm and kept eating. He finished before I did, and as he put his plate in the sink, he told me to go down to the barn when I had finished supper and turn that light out. He said he was going over to visit old man Grimes, and it would probably be late when he got back.

He had told me to do quite a few things in my young life, and this was probably the easiest chore he had ever thought of. Since I knew what the problem was anyway, I said, "Yes sir," and reached for another helping of beans and cornbread. I heard him drive off towards the Grimes place, and I just took my time getting done with my meal.

By the time I got started down to the barn, it was dark and the clouds had pert near blocked out the moon. There was a kind of spooky wind blowing, and I got to thinking of that goofy bullsnake. By the time I reached the barn, I had got plumb spooked myself, and I figured I'd just reach in the door and turn the light off and haul my little nervous butt back to the house.

This barn had been involved in a couple of pretty scary things. Like the time one of the hands walked in on a bobcat, or the time the Old Man walked in on a coyote that was helping itself to one of our cats. Both of these times were at night, and I was willing to bet that the clouds had the moon nearly covered and there was a weird wind blowing.

The barn door was the kind that slid to one side on rollers, and we always left it open a couple of inches so the cats could get in and keep down the mice and things like that. So I walked up to the door, stuck my hand inside along the wall, found the light switch, and turned the light off. I headed pretty quick back to the house and had gone about thirty feet when the light came on.

Now, as you may have guessed, my imagination was what some people call overtaxed. My hair stood up, and I had one of the worst attacks of goosebumps in the history of modern science. I turned very slowly back to the barn and just stared at the door.

I knew for a fact that I had turned the light off so it would stay off, and yet it had come back on. The only thing I could figure was there was a bobcat in there the size of a tiger that had learned how to work a light switch just so he could trap an innocent little kid and dine better than usual.

Something else I figured was that if the Old Man came home and that barn light was still on, I'd be better off if that bad-natured kitty got me instead of him.

I eased back to the barn door. I tried to look in as far as I could and see as much as possible from about ten feet away, but I knew I would have to get closer. I finally got my nerve up and reached inside to shut the light off.

Just as I clicked the switch off, something big and nasty grabbed my hand. I don't mind telling you, I stretched my switch-flicking hand and arm twenty-nine inches, not to mention that I pert near blew out my tonsils when I screamed.

I put up a whale of a fight, but I was losing ground. Whatever had me was dragging me inside the barn, and I did *not* want to go.

Just as whatever-it-was got me inside the barn door, the barn light came on again and the Old Man asked if I thought there'd be any more problem with the light switch.

I'll guarantee you one thing: I was so relieved to know I wasn't going to be eaten by some kind of large wild varmint, I assured him the light switch was *fixed*. In fact, I'd probably never touch another one unless he wanted me to.

Chapter Seven

Cuddles Goes Blind

I hired out to a ranch in Eastern New Mexico one fall, with just fall delivery in mind. But due to the exceptional weather and the fact that I wrecked my pickup and needed more money, I decided to stay on a couple of months longer than my original plans.

I had worked on this particular ranch several times since I was a kid, and I thought quite a lot of the old man who owned it. For that reason, I didn't just blow up and walk out when he asked me to help dig a couple of new water wells.

He explained that I could use the extra money to fix my pickup and even learn how to do something constructive.

Since he was getting up in years, he had hired three more men besides me to dig these wells. I have no idea how old he was, but one of the men he hired was way yonder older-looking than him. He looked like he could have dug Julius Caesar's first water well at his headquarters just west of Rome.

The other two were grown men about my age, eighteen, and—I was to find out—so full of meanness they couldn't hardly sleep at night. They were brothers.

The boss figured we could stay in a line camp on the southwest border of the ranch. That way we would only be a couple of miles from each well.

We finally got the old cabin cleaned out and livable, stored our groceries, got our bedrolls squared away and enough wood cut for supper and breakfast cooking. Since the weather had been warm so far, we didn't get too worried about stocking up on firewood except for cooking.

But the weather in New Mexico held true to form, and about 4:30 the next morning, it started raining, a cold, miserable slow rain with a slight breeze.

That's when Ben, Mark, and myself realized that we had been dealt a cold, miserable hand by Lady Luck.

It seems the old man was not only old but extremely grouchy when he got out of bed and no one had started the fire. He mumbled and growled, sounding like a mad bear, and after he finished cussing all three of us out, he laid down the law. He said if he was going to cook, Mark could chop the firewood and build the fire, I could wash the dishes, and Ben could keep the cabin clean.

That made sense to me, mainly because I could stay in my nice warm bedroll until breakfast was nearly ready.

After I finished the dishes, we headed out to dig a well. Mark, Ben, and I had nicknamed the old man Cuddles, and I'll guarantee you one thing, that was a complete contradiction in terms.

We had been hard at work for about two hours when the cold drizzle turned into a cold downpour. With fifty mile an hour winds. After about a thirty-second discussion, we headed for camp.

On arrival, there was another discussion. It seems there wasn't but two chunks of firewood and our fearless woodcutter had no intention of getting wet chopping more.

After the three of us pointed out he couldn't get any wetter but he could sure get hungrier, he decided to chop wood.

Ben and I helped bring in a load, and Cuddles got a meal going, griping the whole time about getting stuck with a bunch of dumb kids.

After a good meal (Cuddles was a fine cook) and a change of clothes, everyone was warm and in a decent mood for a change, and the rains kept coming.

The next five days were so miserable we couldn't work. All we did was lay around camp, tell lies, and listen to Cuddles gripe.

I repaired some horse gear I had brought with me and used the last of my latigo leather and rawhide lacing to tie up the chairs in that old cabin.

Mark and Ben were constantly aggravating each other and messing with Cuddles. The old man would just cuss and swear if he ever got out of there alive, he was going to go back to preaching.

The afternoon of the sixth day, the boss came up to check on us. He said the rain was general and there was plenty of it. Fact is, he almost didn't make it up there. He said that old power wagon could do just about everything but swim, and by the time he got back to headquarters, he figured it would be able to at least tread water.

He said since all the rains had come, he would wait 'til late spring to dig those two new wells. But we could go on over to the mare pasture and deepen the well over there and see if we could get any water.

He said he brought a set of dominoes for us to use since the weather was bad. He figured they might keep us from killing each other.

Little did he know them dominoes would pert near cause a killing instead of preventing one.

We decided to play some Forty-Two that night. Mark's bed was on the same side of the table and back about six foot from where I sat. Right at the head of the bed close to the door was a bucket of water hauled in for drinking purposes. It was so cold it just about could be called ice.

So we chose pardners and started playing Forty-Two. Cuddles was Mark's pardner and both were good Forty-Two players. Ben and I could keep up, but just barely. After the first hour or so, Cuddles started getting sleepy. Them boys noticed that if we took our time to play, old Cuddles would doze off and he would have to be shook to be woke up.

With the rain coming down outside and one little window in that cabin, the only light came from the two kerosene lamps. The heating stove gave just a small glow from the grated door, but it was burned down to just good hot coals. Beyond the glow of the lamps, it was very dark.

We was into the third trick when Cuddles dozed off. Mark blew out one of the lamps and Ben did the same to the other, and man, it was dark as the inside of a cow. I had no idea what them two idiots was fixing to pull, but I had a feeling it was going to be wild.

Ben reached over and shook Cuddles awake and told him to hurry up and play. Cuddles woke up and then he got spooked.

"My God, I'm blind!" he screamed. "Oh, help me, I cain't see."

Then he started swinging his arms around trying to find someone to help him.

Actually, I couldn't see any more than he could, and I wasn't all that shook up until one of his arms knocked me out of my chair and plumb back over on Mark's bed. While I was headed for the bed, I heard chairs crashing and dominoes going everywhere and some of the loudest laughing I had ever heard in my life.

Cuddles had gone berserk! Screaming and hollering and promising never to drink or cuss again, *anything* if he could just have his sight back. He ran into everything in the cabin, destroying most all of it but the stoves and lamps.

I crawled under the bed and started hollering at Cuddles, trying to tell him he wasn't blind, the lights was out.

Cuddles finally tripped on a chair and landed on the floor next to me. That's when I grabbed him. I finally got him calmed down and quiet, and then we found a lamp and got some light going.

Mark and Ben was holding their sides and their cheeks had tear tracks and they was still giggling when Cuddles got his bearings.

He looked around at the mess and then at the boys. When he looked at me, I just shrugged and stepped back.

Cuddles finally cracked a slight smile and then told Mark and Ben that since they caused the mess, they could clean it up. And if it wasn't cleaned up in five minutes, they would have a diet of oatmeal as long as they was around him.

When everything was back in place and all seemed to be fine, Cuddles walked to the door, picked up that bucket of drinking water and poured half on Mark's bedroll and the other half on Ben's. He was grinning the whole time. Then he went to his room and said good night.

Mark and Ben quit laughing when Cuddles soaked down their beds and then they settled down on the floor with their slickers and coats for a miserable night. Even though the floor was a bad place to try and sleep, I could hear both of them giggling off and on all night.

Chapter Eight

Rutherford the Blind Mule

One morning out at the line camp, the weather was about as nasty and disagreeable as it could be. There was ice everywhere, a slight breeze of thirty or eighty miles per hour, overcast skies, and not a hint of sunshine. The only good thing was it had quit raining.

We went to the first water-well site after breakfast and loaded all of the tools, and then we headed for the mare pasture.

Cuddles was in his usual bad mood, but he had an unusual smirk on his face the whole time he was griping.

It was nerve-wracking enough trying to keep ahead of those two practical jokers, but now I had to contend with a grouchy old man with revenge on his mind.

This was an unusual situation. It was usually me that had everybody else worried, but now I was the innocent bystander. It was driving me smooth up the wall.

We got back to camp about four that evening, got all our chores done, and settled down for the night. That cabin wasn't much, but with a fire going and a good hot meal, it seemed like a mansion.

After I finished with the dishes, I started to work on a headstall I had been plaiting out of rawhide, and Mark and Ben was busy working on a pair of Mark's chaps.

Cuddles appeared at the door to his room and said we had better get our rest because he was figuring on getting an early start and staying late. He wanted to get that old well cleaned out and water in it before the weather got any worse.

The next morning we had our chores done and breakfast ate by five o'clock and was headed for the mare pasture while it was still dark.

When we got to the old dry well, we built a fire and started some coffee. In less than an hour, we were ready to start digging and getting water.

The name of this pasture also told what the pasture was used for. It was strictly for raising horses and for retired horses to live out the rest of their days in good grass and natural cover from the hard winters.

In this pasture was a big bay mule that some of the hands estimated to be thirty years old or older. Anywhere there was fifteen or more colts you could find old Rutherford M. He was a self-appointed babysitter and grass finder for the young colts. He could find water for all, even in the driest of years, and he always led the herd to the best grass.

Rutherford M wasn't only the keeper of the young ones, he was the ace biscuit thief in nine counties. Rutherford M was a chronic beggar. He could smell cold bread fifteen miles away downwind, and he would hang around camp until you changed country. I guess he was the only mule in history to be a certified, grade A, number-one, dyed-in-the-wool *biscuitaholic.*

We had all taken our turn down in the well digging and filling up the buckets and had decided to shut down for a cup of coffee, when we heard the clinking of a bell. It wasn't but just a few minutes until old Rutherford M showed up begging for grub.

Mark and Ben didn't know about Rutherford's problems, and after Cuddles explained the situation, they couldn't have cared less. They seemed to think old Rutherford ought to be sold for soap or shot and fed to the hogs.

Now that made me mad, and as I sat there sipping my coffee, I silently declared war on these two jokers that didn't have any respect for man nor beast. And I had already developed a plan.

Cuddles was the first one back down the hole, and after a spell, I went down and he came up. We had made pretty good progress, and I could hear old Rutherford M walking around, ringing his bell and begging for grub.

When it was time for me to come up, I went cheerfully. I hated being in closed-in places. After I had a quick cup of coffee, I mentioned that if Mark and Ben both would get in the well, we could probably be down to sand and maybe get water by quitting time.

Cuddles looked at me like I had lost my mind. That was a fair-sized hole, but it might be a little crowded with two down there instead of just one. I just nodded at him and winked, and he didn't say anything about it. In fact, he even backed me up, and between the two of us we convinced them to go down and dig.

As soon as they got started, I lured Rutherford M back up to the wagon and gave him what was left of my lunch. I slipped a rope around his neck and tied him up.

Then I took the bell off of his neck and started to the hole, ringing it every step.

One of the boys hollered to keep that stupid blind mule away from the well so he wouldn't walk off into it and crush 'em to death.

Well, old Cuddles caught on quick. He started hollering and clapping his hands like he was driving old Rutherford M away. And I turned and walked away, ringing the bell.

We did this three or four times and each time they thought the mule was getting closer, and each time they screamed a little louder and cussed a little more.

Finally, just about time to quit and they was ready to come up, I picked up the bell and headed for the well. I also got a coat out of the wagon.

They started hollering again and Cuddles started acting like he was trying to drive old Rutherford M off. But I just kept gettin closer and closer. As I got to the edge of the well, I hollered, "Look out, he's gonna fall in." I kicked a little dirt in and then threw in the coat and the bell.

From there on things got pretty exciting for them two.

Cuddles and me couldn't see what was happening but we could sure hear it. There was a couple of rather terrifying screams, followed by bumps and thuds and cussing. And then silence. Well, semi-silence. You couldn't have heard a cannon go off for the noise that Cuddles was making with his laughing.

To make matters worse for our boys below, water started coming into the well.

After Mark and Ben got over their scare and realized they were standing in water, they decided to come on up out of there.

They was almost to the top when Cuddles stopped 'em cold.

Before he would let them out, one of them had to go back down and get the bell, and then he made 'em promise not to pull any more jokes on him or me. They about had all they could stand, so they agreed. Cuddles let 'em out.

It was dark by the time we got the tower back up and the pipe centered. When the little Aeromotor finally got to pumping and we had water coming, I put the bell back on Rutherford M and we headed back to camp.

Mark and Ben was pretty quiet all the way back. They didn't eat much supper and everyone had a good night's sleep.

The next morning Mark and Ben quit. Cuddles and me hauled them back to headquarters and said our good-byes.

Everyone at headquarters had a good laugh when Cuddles explained how Mark and Ben got so black and blue and why they quit.

The boss said he didn't need any more wells dug, but if I wanted to, I could take fifteen of his three- and four-year colts back up to that camp and ride 'em for thirty to forty-five days. And if I thought I could get along with Cuddles, he could go along to ride fence and feed when he needed to.

I agreed pretty quick, and so did Cuddles.

After all we had been through, we both was looking forward to some nice quiet days handling unbroke horses.

Bifocals and Store-Bought Teeth

The year R.V. turned forty-six he started going downhill, sort of like a runaway freight train.

Naturally, I tried to help him adapt by giving him little tidbits of encouragement, especially after he finally admitted his teeth had been bothering him and that he might need to get his eyes checked. He admitted this after he took too many steps and fell into the kitchen door.

By the time R.V.'s wife and me got him untangled from the screen door, she had decided that he was going to get his eyes checked. He said he'd get his eyes checked when he was good and ready. Just because a man stumped his toe didn't mean he was going blind.

She informed him that he was ready, whether he liked it or not.

As I started inside the house, I noticed a tooth laying right there in the doorway, where there used to be a screen door. The ugly thing looked pretty dry, so I figured that whoever lost it had been keeping it in his shirt pocket in hopes of meeting the tooth fairy in person.

I mentioned this to R.V. as I handed him the tooth. I figured it was his tooth, 'cause he was first in the house, I was second, and them other two hands was still carrying what was left of the screen door out to the trash pit.

The look I got from R.V. could've killed a charging bull at forty paces. He was about to talk to me about the size of my mouth when his wife stepped in.

"That's right, you've lost three teeth in three weeks. When are you going to go to the dentist and find out what's wrong?" Then to me. "He hasn't been able to eat anything more solid than cornbread soaked in milk for the last four days, and I generally have to crumble up the cornbread because he can't see good enough to get it in the glass."

"I wish you'd talk some sense into the ironheaded old thing, because if he doesn't get some kind of help, I'm going to go stay with my mother 'til he either gets better or dies. I mean it, somebody better do something, and fast!"

Well, R.V. said he didn't want to see a dentist and didn't need an eye doctor, and just to prove it, on his way out the door he ran smooth over the icebox.

His wife called that afternoon for an appointment with the eye doctor. What she didn't tell R.V. was that she called a dentist, too.

After a week, R.V.'s glasses came in and he'd had all his choppers pulled out. To say he was a little grouchy would be an understatement. He and his wife went into town to get him measured for the dentures and then to get him fitted into his new bifocals. His wife hurried the old pickup towards town, driving with one hand and keeping R.V. from jumping out with the other.

They got back just after dark, and I went over to check on R.V. As I walked into the kitchen, I noticed he was looking a little ragged. Fact is, he looked like he had stuck his head into a sack full of bobcats. His wife explained why he looked so bad.

When he got his new glasses, he could actually *see*. He was so tickled, he could hardly stand it, and as usual, he wasn't listening when the doctor tried to warn him about them little squares at the bottom of his lenses.

So when they left the doctor's office, R.V. didn't bother to open the glass door, he just walked through it. Seems that when he looked through them little squares, the bar across the door appeared to be just a hair farther out than it really was.

It only took six stitches in his knee and about a quart of iodine and two band-aids on his head. His wife was kind of grinning when she finished up by saying, "At least it got his mind off the fact that he didn't have a tooth left in his head."

After a couple of days, R.V. was ready to get his new teeth. His exact words were, "When I get them store-bought choppers in, we're coming back here and I'm eating the biggest steak on this ranch, with plenty of fried potatoes and onions."

As the two of them was getting in the pickup to go to town, I promised them I would cook supper, even though the dentist had already told him that it would be a while before he could eat like a normal person. I promised him I would have his steak done just like he wanted it.

Supper was a wreck.

After trying to chew that first bite of steak for twenty minutes, he decided to try the fried potatoes and onions. They were softer than the steak but they stuck his uppers to his lowers, and both uppers and lowers followed his fork back to the plate.

I hardly ever laughed at a man's embarrassment, but this time I slipped. While he was trying to get his teeth off the fork, I told him that maybe he should just put a chunk of meat in them choppers, run 'em by hand, then pick up the meat, pop it in his mouth and swallow it. It made sense to me.

For the next week, we were fixing fence and getting the last little things ready to start receiving cattle. This meant that R.V.'s wife had to make our lunches every day, and me and the other two hands was making bets on what R.V. would bring for his noontime nourishment.

The next day when we shut down for dinner, me and the two hands had steak sandwiches, iced tea, and canned peaches. R.V.'s wife had fixed him two sandwiches and kept them separate from ours. She had cut up his steak in little bite-sized chunks and placed them on the bread.

He sat down with a cup of tea and started tearing off one bite at a time. It was taking him a while but he was managing to get everything chewed up and washed down.

As he finished up his first sandwich, I said, "Why don't you start using them teeth like they're supposed to be used? While it's just us out here, you ought to try a regular sandwich. If anything goes wrong, nobody will know but us."

R.V. agreed. He reached for another sandwich, unwrapped it, examined it through his new glasses, and very carefully brought it to his mouth. Then with the confidence of an all-pro tackle, he attacked.

He bit plumb through the first finger on his right hand. He tried to scream but all he could do was roar and

blow crumbs. It's hard to express true feelings when you got a mouth full of teeth, steak, and finger. So as a last resort, he just jerked.

He not only got his finger back but he jerked his teeth out. As he drove off, and left us rolling around on the ground, he pitched his teeth out the pickup window and tossed his glasses up on the dash.

After a while R.V. got so's he could see with his glasses and chew with his store-bought teeth. Now, if I can just find my glasses, I'm going to throw a cast iron skillet at that sick-minded kid of mine who keeps passing me the gravy and grinning.

Payback is a terrible thing.

Chapter Ten

A Bronc in the Clothesline

I've learned to patch quite a few things so they'll work for a while, but I'm just not into complete and total repair like some of the more mechanical-minded hombres I have known.

Since I was about sixteen years old, I have figured if it can't be done a-horseback, someone else needs to be hired to do it. This attitude has helped me cover a lot of country while hunting jobs.

When the Little Woman and I moved to a certain ranch in New Mexico, things were in a little disrepair, and the clothesline was one item that the Little Woman just couldn't accept.

The wooden T-posts had been in the ground since Shep was a pup and were rotten from top to bottom. The first old Levis and shirts put on the lines were too much for 'em to stand.

When I came in from the pasture that evening, I was informed there would be new posts and new wire pretty quick or I would be out the expense of a new electric dryer.

Now, I'm not tight, just conservative. I scrounged around and found an old telephone pole that had been broke off, and I proceeded to make a clothes line pole. The biggest trouble was, by the time I got everything cut, nailed, and squared up, I only had enough free lumber for one end of the clothesline.

Well, I figured I could use one wall of the well house for the other end of the clothesline. By the time I got the telephone-end set down pretty deep and the wires run through the wall and anchored by a cedar stay, I didn't have a pretty good clothesline, I had one that would last forever.

After I convinced the Little Woman it wouldn't kill her to walk an extra seventy or eighty feet to hang out a few pieces of laundry, she quit screaming and let me in the house. It didn't bother me all that much to cook my own meals for a day or two.

But she finally realized I knew what I was talking about. She could get some exercise and have time to think about all the other things she needed to be doing.

Well, one morning I had a four-year old colt go to bucking with me just as we started past the well house. I had decided to take a short cut.

This colt blows up and proceeds to destroy everything in his path. I'm not a bucking-horse rider and I never have been, but this one time I managed to set there and get this powder-headed idiot pulled up.

Wouldn't you know it, the only time I get a decent bronc ride going and the bronc I'm trying to ride bucks under the clothesline, which I had forgotten about because I was so tickled to be riding this pitching horse and doing a pretty fair job of it.

I remembered the clothesline just about the time that clabber-minded colt bucked around the corner of the well house and hung the saddle horn on the first wire.

When all the weight of that colt and me hit the clothesline, it kind of tested the durability of the well house wall and my telephone pole. The telephone pole was a little stouter.

When that wall came exploding out, the goofy colt spooked. When he tried to run off, he raised his head just enough to catch the fourth wire under his jaw while the other three were caught on the saddle horn.

I've been around a wreck or two, and when this 'un started, I figured out right quick that I needed to be somewhere besides where I was. I bailed out just in time to get run over by a big chunk of plaster, two-by-fours, and the electrical box.

The Little Woman had just come from the house with a basket of wet clothes. She showed no concern that I could've been killed, or that I had pert near rode that colt. She said something about all the sparks them bare electrical wires was causing and that she'd be more than glad to use 'em to sear the scratches on my head.

When I finally got out from under what was left of the wall, I told her not to worry, I'd get an electrician out and have the well house back in working order by that afternoon, even though it might be a day or two before I could get the wall replaced.

"You'd better get someone out here NOW to fix that electricity, and while you're calling, you call someone to fix that wall, and I mean today."

When I asked her if she would help me catch that colt, she gave me a really strange look. I didn't understand exactly what she said I could do with the colt, but I did hear her mention that I would probably have him caught by the time she got back from town *with her new dryer.*

71

It's pretty tough to get someone that's got any knowledge of electrical things to travel thirty-two miles on short notice, but after begging and promising to pay time-and-a-half, I got an old boy to come out and fix the power supply line for our water pump.

This electrical specialist got there about the same time the Little Woman got back from town. I noticed she didn't have anything in the back of the pickup, and I just naturally figured she had come to her senses and decided she could still use a clothesline.

I was so tickled, I just had to run up and tell her.

She turned on me so fast it's a wonder she didn't get a nose bleed. She informed me that the dryer was on its way out and that she had hired some guys to bring it and install it, just to make sure that it worked right. And if I wanted to sleep in the comfort of my own home, I had better stay out of the way.

All that high-dollar technical help finally got finished about six that evening, and when they left out, I eased into the house to see how things were going.

The dryer people had to knock out part of the storeroom wall to make room for the dryer, and the electrical people had to run a new line to the storeroom, and the whole place was one big mess. The Little Woman was in the process of getting things cleaned up, and I was hungry.

When I asked her why she didn't have supper ready, I noticed a little wisp of smoke coming from her right ear. I hollered from the back yard that I would be glad to fix supper for her since she was so tired. I would even help with the dishes if she wanted me to. Didn't work.

Along about nine that evening, I slipped into the kitchen and fixed me a snack. And while I was eating, I finally got things figured out.

The next time she tried to force me into some common labor, I would remind her about the way things turned out the time I built her a clothesline, and the next time a colt started bucking with me, I would let him buck me off. A man needs to keep things as normal as possible.

Chapter Eleven

Good Help Is Hard To Find

Once, just before the Fourth of July rodeo, I had a set of leathers go bad in a windmill in the west pasture. Normally I would have just moved some cattle around and fixed the well after the roping, but I had just put some straightened-out yearlings in there and I needed all the fresh water I could get.

Since all the neighbors were tied up with their own problems or already gone to some of the rodeos scattered around the country, I figured me and the Little Woman could pull the rods and have the well pumping by late afternoon. I mean, it was only the second and I wasn't up in the steer roping until the afternoon of the third. With the Little Woman helping me, I had plenty of time.

The Little Woman is probably the best cook west of the Mississippi, and she can make a shirt better than any professional tailor, but at times she can get plumb snarly. She don't take orders worth a rip, and she *sure* don't take constructive criticism.

After I rode back to the house and got the tools loaded in the pickup, I finally convinced her to come help me. Since it was a shallow well, I figured I could pull it by hand while she set the wrenches. Well, I finally got the Little

Woman and old Jughead (my pitbull–Queensland heeler crossbred cowdog pup) loaded up. Since we only had to go through eight gates, I let her drive, mainly because her and that pup had never learned to shut a gate properly. It was about 11:30 in the morning when we finally got to the well. After I got everything loose and ready to go, I adjusted the wrenches and explained to her what I wanted her to do.

Jughead jumped out of the pickup and laid down in the shade. That dog was showing more and more sense all the time.

I got started pulling on the rods, and by the time I finally got the top check out of the cylinder, I thought my hemorrhoids had hemorrhoids. I got to the first coupling and told her to put the wrench on the bottom rod and pull up on the handle. I set the weight of the rods on the wrench, let the wrench rest on the top of the pipe, broke the top rod loose, and stood it in the corner of the tower. I thought to myself, "This may go a lot better than I figured."

That was about the only good thought I had for the rest of the day.

Two rods later, Jughead figured he would get in on the act. He came charging into the tower and jumped up on the Little Woman's leg so's he could get a better look. He not only got a better look, he scared the Little Woman. She screamed, spooked me, and I dropped the rods.

I commented on the fact that Jughead was something to really be scared of. After all, he was all of eight months old and he had been known on occasion to maul a warm buttered biscuit.

She mentioned that since I was so big, bad, and brave, and always had total control, I could run those rods back in the well and fish the others out. I started wondering if there might be any tourists at the coffee shop in town.

Well, I run the rest of the rods in, got tied on to the ones I had dropped, and started pulling 'em out again. By not we had a pretty good audience. About two hundred steers, thirty antelope, and a double handful of jack rabbits.

I put Jughead in the back of the pickup to avoid a major wreck with the steers. You know how aggressive a cowdog pup can be. I unseated the top check again, and this time we had all but three of the rods out.

The Little Woman happened to look around and see the antelope. I wouldn't have minded her taking time to appreciate the local wildlife, but she happened to notice the critters at the same time I thought she had hooked the rods.

Have you ever heard three rods speeding to the bottom of a one-hundred-forty-foot well? They didn't make near the noise I did. I raised my voice a little.

I mentioned to the Little Woman that she had better keep her mind on her work or things could get a little rough. When I finally got her to put the wrench down, I climbed down off the tower and started running rods back in the well.

There is an old saying, the third time is the charm. And this time it held true. We finally got all the rods out. the new Blackjack leather on and all the rods back in the well. I think the reason we got along so good on this trip was we were both so mad we didn't say hardly anything; we just worked. But as I started to hook up the redrod, things got out of hand.

During the run back to the bottom, the steers got to thinking they needed a closer look at what was going on. They had eased up all around the windmill tower, just to watch the Little Woman and myself struggle to get them water. While they was watching us, Jughead was watching them. I was watching my step and the Little Woman was watching for more antelope.

One steer was watching Jughead and that's all it took. When that steer tried to smell of Jughead, Jughead bit him on the end of the nose and then forgot to turn the steer loose (the pit in him).

Now, one steer running backwards with a dog on the end of his nose is pretty spooky to the other one hundred ninety-nine that's standing around minding their own business. Especially if the dog's growling, the steer's bellowing, and the Little Woman's screaming.

When about half the steers bumped the tower, I fell off the guide boards. About the time I hit the ground, the Little Woman bailed off into the water tank. Seems she saw Jughead and that steer coming. They broke through the bottom brace on the tower and came inside with me.

I don't care what anyone says, it only takes one steer, one dog, and one mad woman to have a stampede.

I grabbed Jughead's hind legs and pert near ripped that steer's lips off.

When the steer got rid of all that unwanted weight and pain, he paused for just a second. When he saw me and the furry little critter that bit him, he turned and joined the Little Woman in the water tank.

Of course the Little Woman was in the process of coming back to surface and she didn't see her swimming companion take the dive. That crossbred steer hit the Little Woman right square in the hip pockets.

I didn't know what to do first, kill the dog or help the Little Woman out of the water tank. It only took a couple of seconds to make the decision. I turned the dog loose and ran. I could tell she wasn't hurt by the way she was chasing Jughead and swinging that wrench.

I told her if she would just calm down, I would drive her to the house. She informed me she didn't want to calm down and she could drive herself to the house.

What was the last straw, as she got in the pickup and started to leave, that traitor of a dog jumped in the back just as she was pulling out.

As they bumped out of sight, I turned the windmill on and gathered up what tools I could find and stacked them inside the tower. Then I started walking home.

It wasn't all that bad, because this way I could still make the roping and know for sure that all the gates was shut properly. And in spite of the help situation, I had water in my west pasture.

Chapter Twelve

Springtime in the Sands

Springtime in the sandhills can be a little spooky. The mesquite and other plants take a turn for the better, and even though it's been pretty dry, everything has a green tint to it. Of course, things get worse if we've had any moisture to speak of.

By worse, I mean things that grow get really green and all the little sneaky varmints that live in all that green stuff start to move around a little.

If we should keep getting rain, most of those critters start to hunt for dryer ground. I have found snakes in the garage, in the feed room, and even under the hood of the Little Woman's car. The one under the hood was trying to imitate a fan belt, and was permanently dead, but still he caused considerable excitement.

If I'd had any idea as to what I would find when I started tracing down that smell, I'd have taken the car to the local filling station and flat-fixing place. But no, not me. I figured the smell came from a burned coil wire mixed with a slightly scorched air cleaner, so I attacked.

Dead or not, a twenty-nine-foot bullsnake will scare you when you sneak up on him. He was probably not that long til he got stretched around the waterpump pulley.

I casually mentioned to the Little Woman that the next time she smelled something like that, she needed to take it to the gas station to get it checked. It's cheaper than buying medicine to help patch up all the skinned places a man can get just trying to get away from a dead snake.

It hadn't been too good a year for me. Jobs were scarce, and I hadn't been doing too good at team roping— or anything else, as far as that goes. It seemed the only thing that had gone even close to right was our girls softball team. My daughter was playing and I was coach. The Little Woman was the team chaperon, and Jughead was the team mascot. Somehow we had managed to get into the play-offs for the championship.

To give you an idea of how things were going for me, I got knocked out by a renegade pitch from a thirteen-year-old girl the first night of the play-offs. I had a black eye and one fine headache the next morning, and we still had four more days to go.

Our team was scheduled for a two-game day, one early in the afternoon and then one at 9:45 at night. So the Little Woman figures we can buy sandwich makings and save several bucks on meals. I'm all for it.

We get cleaned up and head into town, stop at the grocery store, and she goes in and buys all kinds of swell stuff for our meal. It's one of those places where you have to sack your own groceries.

Now, anyone who's ever picked up a paper sack knows how to open one. You just grab one side and pop it open. And if it's done right, it not only scares the fool out of the person next to you, but it is ready for anything you should want to put in it.

The Little Woman grabbed the sack and tried to pop it open a little too hard. When she popped it, the sack tore out of her hand, ricocheted off an innocent push basket, and flew back and hit her right square in the eye.

I was sitting in the pickup with our daughter and old Jughead when the manager of the store escorted the Little Woman and her cart of groceries out to us.

She was a little upset, not so much at being helped out to the pickup, but at the fact I mentioned she shouldn't have been messing around with such high-tech equipment. Her eye was watering pretty good, but she didn't want to go to the doctor. So we got out the first aid kit and the water can and rigged her a patch for the time being.

By the time our first ball game was just about over, her eye had started hurting pretty bad, and I was getting worried about her.

As soon as the game was done, we left all the groceries with the assistant coach, and I hauled the Little Woman to the doctor.

After a quick check, the doctor found a place that the sack had cut and took care of it like a pro. He informed us she would be fine in a day or two, but she would have to keep medication on it and wear a patch.

We got back to the ball park in plenty of time for all the girls to pert near ruin the poor old silly thing with kindness. They never treated me like that when I got molested by a runaway pitch. Fact is, I think all that attention was the main reason we lost the game that night. And losing the game put us up the next evening around 6:00.

We made a cute couple, me with a black eye and her with one good one, but we made it home and got a fairly good night's sleep.

The next day, I practiced roping for about three hours and worked my horses pretty hard and then went in to clean up and get ready for our last game. The Little Woman stayed inside and tried to keep from straining her eye.

I got the water just right, stepped in the shower, closed the glass doors, and lathered up. It was after everything had steamed up and I was fixing to get down to some serious singing that I noticed I had a visitor—a little slithery-type visitor about forty feet long.

I tried to jump back. Didn't work. Seems there was a wall back there. Since I couldn't run, I figured I would just catch the slimy little varmint. I guess he had some soap in his eyes from coming up the drain, because he didn't seem very upset until I reached for him.

At first I thought he was a bullsnake, but when I reached for him I kind of disturbed him, and he coiled and started rattling. I gave him the shower. Or I should say, I *tried* to give him the shower. The only time in ten years those glass doors wouldn't open on their own, and *this* time they were stuck permanent.

Contrary to popular belief, a two hundred twenty-five pound man can hang from a set of wet, slippery glass doors and a wet and slippery tile wall by his toes, while screaming for someone to bring him a shovel or hoe or anything to kill a soapy rattlesnake.

I screamed for the Little Woman to bring me a shovel or hoe.

"What do you want?"

"I want a shovel or hoe."

"Why do you want a shovel or a hoe? You're not that dirty."

"BRING ME A SHOVEL OR A HOE!"

"Why?" By now she's getting as mad as I am scared.

"Cause there's a rattlesnake in the tub with me!"

"There isn't any snake in the tub with you!"

Zane, our daughter, got in on the act. "What's daddy screaming about?"

"Oh, he thinks there is a snake in the bathtub with him."

Zane mentioned something about getting hit with that ball hadn't helped me any, when I squalled again that I wanted a shovel or a hoe.

By now Jughead is barking and making the snake nervous. The snake is touring the bathtub, and I'm about to have a litter of kittens.

Well, the Little Woman sends Zane out to get a shovel and she comes feeling her way into the bathroom, just to see what's going on. In our bathroom, the toilet is pretty close to the bathtub, and the shower doors go to about eight inches from the ceiling. So the Little Woman wallers up on the toilet seat and tries to stick her head over the shower doors to see what's going on. She finally adjusts herself so's she can see with her good eye, looks in, and says, "My God, Curt, there's a snake in there with you!"

After chopping the critter into umpteen pieces, I couldn't tell whether I was wet from sweating or the shower.

Needless to say, as soon as I got the mess cleaned up, I put a screen over the hose coming from the bathtub drain out in the backyard.

We finally made the game, and I'm not sure how, but within a matter of minutes people knew I had shared my shower with a snake. You'd be surprised how many unfeeling people there are in this world.

We won the game, finishing third for the season, and I was pretty proud until some of the girls came up with their parents and introduced me as the coach who thought rubber ducks were out.

Curt Brummett's work has appeared in *Team Ropers Times, DeBaca County News, Livestock Weekly*, and *Horse and Rider*. He and his wife Sheila live in Maljamar, New Mexico. They have three daughters (Debbie, Dana, and Zane) and three grandchildren (Joe, Lonesome, and Justa).

Humor from August House Publishers

Cowboy Folk Humor
Jokes, tall tales, and anecdotes about cowboys, their pranks, their foibles, and their times.
ISBN 0-87483-104-0, PB, $8.95

A Field Guide to Southern Speech
A twenty-gauge lexicon for the duck blind, the deer stand, the skeet shoot, the bass boat, and the backyard barbecue.
ISBN 0-87483-098-2, PB, $6.95

Gridiron Grammar
A handbook to understanding coaches, players, officials, Monday-morning quarterbacks, and football widows in the South.
ISBN 0-87483-158-X, TBP, $6.95

Laughter in Appalachia
Appalachia's special brand of humor—dry, colorful, and earthy—from Loyal Jones and Billy Edd Wheeler.
ISBN 0-87483-031-1, HB, $19.95
ISBN 0-87483-032-X, PB, $8.95

The Night of the Possum Concert
"Charles Allbright has a fine comic touch like no one else I know." —*Charles Portis* "The man is funny, very funny." —*Phil Thomas, Associated Press*
ISBN 0-87483-028-1, PB, $8.95

Gravely the Mules Stopped Dancing
"Allbright writes in the tradition of the Southern humorists, but he outshines them all in his ability to make his readers feel good about other people." —*Dee Brown*
ISBN 0-87483-063-X, HB, $19.95
ISBN 0-87483-062-1, PB, $8.95

The Consecrated Cross-eyed Bear
Stories from the less-solemn side of church life. More humor from Charles Allbright.
ISBN 0-87483-159-8, PB, $8.95

Midwestern Folk Humor
"Here in the land of beer, cheese, and sausage—where the polka is danced and winters are unending and where Lutherans and

Catholics predominate—everybody is ethnic,
the politics are clean, and the humor plentiful."
ISBN 0-87483-108-3, HB, $24.95
ISBN 0-87483-107-5, PB, $11.95

Listening for the Crack of Dawn

A master storyteller recalls the Appalachia of his youth. "A delight-
ful memoir—warm and bittersweet, at times humorous and at
other times heartrending." —*Library Journal*
ISBN 0-87483-153-9, HB, $17.95
ISBN 0-87483-139-X, PB, $9.95

Curing the Cross-Eyed Mule

More from Jones and Wheeler—450 Appalachian jokes, along with
essays by Roy Blount, Jr., and William Lightfoot.
ISBN 0-87483-083-4, PB, $8.95

The Preacher Joke Book

A surprisingly reverent collection of religious humor, poking fun
less at the message than at the messengers.
ISBN 0-87483-087-7, PB, $6.95

Outhouse Humor

Jokes, stories, and songs in tribute to the
"little brown shack out back."
ISBN 0-87483-058-3, PB, $5.95

Dog Tales

Some tall, some true, all collected from the oral tradition, these
stories do justice to our beloved canine friends.
Just right for reading aloud.
ISBN 0-87483-076-1, PB, $6.95

Ozark Tall Tales

Authentic mountain stories as hill folk
have told them for generations.
ISBN 0-87483-099-0, PB, $8.95

AUGUST HOUSE PUBLISHERS
P.O. Box 3223, Little Rock, Arkansas 72203
1-800-284-8784

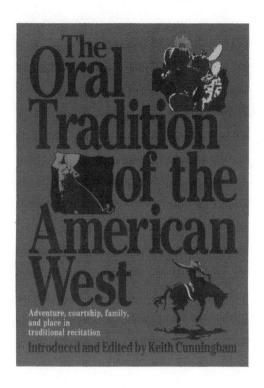

The Oral Tradition of the American West

Adventure, courtship, family, and place in traditional recitation

Introduced and Edited by Keith Cunningham

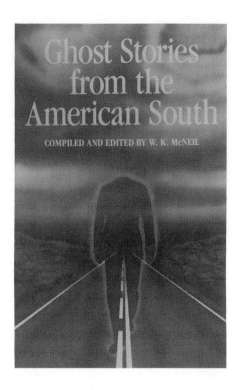

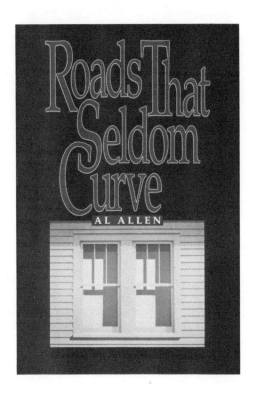

ROADS THAT SELDOM CURVE
Growing up along the Mississippi

"A significant contribution to the literature of remembrance. Allen's
retrospective vision is both mystical and poetic."
—*Jack Farris*

Hardback $19.95 and paperback $9.95